Children of the World

Philippines

For their help in the preparation of *Children of the World: Philippines*, the editors gratefully thank Emraida Kiram, Milwaukee; the Embassy of the Philippines (Canada), Ottawa, Ont.; the Embassy of the Philippines (US), Washington, DC; the International Institute of Wisconsin, Milwaukee; the Canadian Department of Employment and Immigration, Ottawa, Ont.; the US Immigration and Naturalization Service, Press Office, Washington, DC; the United States Department of State, Bureau of Public Affairs, Office of Public Communication, Washington, DC, for unencumbered use of material in the public domain.

Library of Congress Cataloging-in-Publication Data

Bjener, Tamiko.
  Philippines.

  (Children of the world)
  Bibliography: p.
  Includes index.
  Summary: Presents the life of a twelve-year-old boy living in a Philippine fishing town, describing his family, home, school, and amusements and some of the traditions and celebrations of his country.
  1. Philippines—Juvenile literature. 2. Children—Philippines—Juvenile literature. [1. Philippines—Social life and customs. 2. Family life—Philippines] I. Sherwood, Rhoda. II. Knowlton, MaryLee, 1946-III. Sachner, Mark, 1948- . IV. Title. V. Series: Children of the world (Milwaukee, Wis.)
DS655.B54 1987   959.9'046   86-42805
ISBN 1-55532-192-5
ISBN 1-55532-167-4 (lib. bdg.)

North American edition first published in 1987 by

Gareth Stevens, Inc.   7221 West Green Tree Road
Milwaukee, Wisconsin 53223, USA

This work was originally published in shortened form consisting of section I only.

Typeset by Ries Graphics ltd., Milwaukee.
Design: Laurie Shock and Leanne Dillingham.
Map design: Gary Moseley.

1 2 3 4 5 6 7 8 9 92 91 90 89 88 87

Children of the World

Philippines

Photography by
Tamiko Bjener

Edited by
Rhoda Sherwood,
MaryLee Knowlton, &
Mark J. Sachner

Gareth Stevens Publishing
Milwaukee

...a note about *Children of the World:*

The children of the world live in fishing towns and urban centers, on islands and in mountain valleys, on sheep ranches and fruit farms. This series follows one child in each country through the pattern of his or her life. Candid photographs show the children with their families, at school, at play, and in their communities. The text describes the dreams of the children and, often through their own words, tells how they see themselves and their lives.

Each book also explores events that are unique to the country in which the child lives, including festivals, religious ceremonies, and national holidays. The *Children of the World* series does more than tell about foreign countries. It introduces the children of each country and shows readers what it is like to be a child in that country.

...and about *Philippines:*

Elberto has been a fisherman since he was eight years old. When he's not in school he goes out twice a day - at four in the morning and four in the afternoon. Life is a challenge and a joy for this twelve-year-old boy from a land that has changed so much and yet remains unchanged in so many ways.

To enhance this book's value in libraries and classrooms, comprehensive reference sections include up-to-date data about the Philippines' geography, demographics, language, currency, education, culture, industry, and natural resources. *Philippines* also features a bibliography, research topics, activity projects, and discussions of such subjects as Manila, the country's history, political system, ethnic and religious composition, and language.

The living conditions and experiences of children in the Philippines vary tremendously according to economic, environmental, and ethnic circumstances. The reference sections help bring to life for young readers the diversity and richness of the culture and heritage of the Philippines. Of particular interest are discussions of the Philippines' political factions and of the many minority cultures and national groups that have made their presence felt in the nation's language and traditions.

CONTENTS

LIVING IN THE PHILIPPINES:
Elberto, a Young Fisherman

ako hi Elberto Comeo

"Hello. I'm Elberto Comeo."

Elberto Comeo is 12 years old. He lives in San Roque, a fishing village on the Pacific Ocean side of the island of Leyte. Leyte is in the Visayan Islands, one of the Philippines' three largest land areas. There are 3000 villagers in San Roque, many of them children. Leyte is the eighth largest of the 7000 islands in the Philippines. During World War II, fierce fighting took place between the US and Japan. Many villagers were killed in the battles.

North America

South America

Europe

Africa

Asia

— Philippines

Australia

Republic of the Philippines

South China Sea

Pacific Ocean

Manila

Leyte

Sulu Sea

Elberto,
a young fisherman.

Fishing for a Living

Elberto's father, like his grandfather and great-grandfather, is a fisherman. Since he was eight, Elberto too has been fishing. He was put into a boat as a baby so he would learn not to get seasick.

Fishing boats leave the village at 4:00 a.m. and 4:00 p.m., unless the sea is rough. Fishermen row for three hours each trip. If Elberto is not in school, he goes with his father in their boat, called a *banca*. It looks like a canoe with wooden poles on the sides that keep it from tipping over. A boat with poles like these is an outrigger.

Elberto laughs at a fish that is too small to keep.

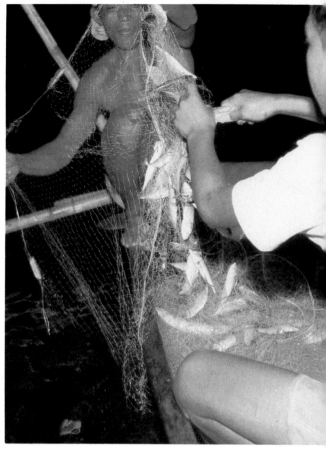

Getting the fish out of the nets is a tough job.

Elberto loves to row and fish. He especially likes the thrill of a big catch. But his job is hard work, too. Often he cuts his fingers on sharp fish fins or gets them pinched by a crab or even a fish that bites.

Elberto fishes in both the ocean and the river. Fishing in the river is harder than fishing in the ocean. Elberto and his father must wade into the river up to their waists. Sometimes they work from five in the afternoon until four in the morning. Those days they get little sleep, but river fish bring in good money.

Sometimes Elberto and his father sell the fish on the beach. But usually they take it to the nearby market. Elberto doesn't keep all his money. He gives it to his mother so she can buy rice. She returns some for his pocket money, which he uses to buy candy and cookies.

At the local market. Elberto's family sells sardines, mullet, flatfish, goby, grouper, tuna, hairtail, needlefish, mackerel, sea bass, sea bream, cuttlefish, prawn, and crabs.

Elberto's father repairs his net in his spare time. Elberto watches so he can learn.

Elberto and his father shop for pieces of net. They buy small pieces that will slowly add up to make their net bigger.

Most Filipino fishermen are like Elberto's father. They have small boats and small nets. They usually have good luck with their fishing. But lately the water has begun to change color. The villagers now call it "red tides." These "red tides" result from wastes dumped into the sea from foreign-owned factories. The fishermen worry. Their lives depend on fishing, and if pollution kills the fish, they will have no way to earn a living.

Elberto sorts out the net.

Everyone is interested when a catch comes in.

Elberto's family. In back: Elberto's father. Second row: Elberto's grandmother, his mother, Norbert, and Elberto.   Middle: Manuel and Facino. Front: Edna, Elba, and Helen. Bottom: Mario, who works in Manila.

Elberto's Family

Elberto has four brothers and three sisters. He is the third boy. Mario, his oldest brother, no longer lives at home. After graduating from school, Mario took a job as a guard in Manila, the capital city. Elberto's grandmother, who worked in town as a maid, has returned to live with the family. Such a large family cannot live on the money earned by selling fish. So Elberto's father drives a pedicab when he is not fishing. A pedicab is a bicycle or motorcycle with a seat attached for passengers. It serves as a taxi for Filipinos.

Jijin, the pig, squirms when he is washed, so it takes Elberto two hours to finish.

Norbert and Elberto fix the pedicab.

Elberto washes clothes.

Little Edna fetches water.

Elberto likes the crowded and noisy home he shares with his brothers, sisters, parents, and grandmother. All the children work. Elberto and his brother Norbert take turns driving the pedicab and fishing. The younger children help cook, sell ice candy, and carry water from the village well.

Elberto drives the pedicab.

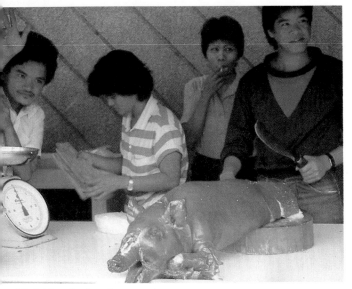
Weighing *lechon* for a customer.

Children mind this sari sari store.

This sari sari store is in front of the school.

The family has two pigs, Jijin and Didin, that live under the floor of Elberto's home. Everyone handles them carefully, especially Elberto, who must give them a bath every day. They do not like baths. After they reach a good size, the pigs are sold. Then they are roasted whole for a dish called *lechon*, a food served at festivals. The whole family enjoys lechon.

Elberto also enjoys the *sari sari* store, a corner variety store found in all Philippine villages. Here, like other children, he uses his pocket money to buy candy.

The family at home, before bedtime.

Today father caught only three small fish and a prawn, so the family uses the fish to make soup, adding *malunggay*, an herb similar to parsley. The soup is poured over rice, an important part of the Filipino diet. Food is cooked over a fire heated by logs.

When there are no other side dishes, the family eats brown sugar or coconut with their soup. It is traditional to eat with one's hands, but some people use spoons and forks. Sometimes guests from far away or Catholic sisters from the nearby convent come to visit families in the village. Filipinos are warm and generous to guests. So if a family has nothing to eat, someone must run to relatives and friends to get food and dishes for the guests.

Norbert makes fish soup over the log fire.

Dishes for a guest. Clockwise from far left: papaya, fish broiled in soy, seaweed, vinegar, fried chicken, crab, rice, and taro leaves cooked in coconut milk.

Mealtime in Elberto's family.

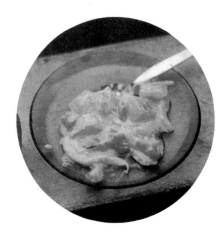

Dessert made with coconut meat.

The boys read a borrowed comic book.

Elberto, like many Filipinos, loves basketball.

The "milk" from the coconut quenches Elberto's thirst.

Coconut — The Tree of Life

Elberto's father has planted three coconut trees in the back garden. The coconut has so many uses that it is called "the tree of life." It is a lucky tree to Filipinos. An old saying is that "if you possess 10 of them you should never be troubled by hard times." Elberto jokes that his family needs only seven more coconut trees to become wealthy.

Golden coconuts from "the tree of life."

The shells of the coconuts are removed, leaving the kernel for copra.

Because it gives so much to the people, the coconut is also known as "the supermarket." People can drink the sweet liquid inside the shell. They can eat the meat of the coconut as it is, or grate it. When crushed or grated, it provides coconut oil, or "coconut milk," for flavoring. Dried coconut, called *copra,* is valuable. The Philippines sell more copra than any country in the world. Filipinos also use copra oil in margarine, soap, and candles.

Machines take out the white kernel of the coconut. The kernel may be used in cooking. When crushed or grated, it gives coconut oil, or "coconut milk."

Villagers use the coconut shells for firewood or charcoal, the trunk of the tree for wood, and the sap for vinegar and *tuba*, which is a kind of wine. Even the leaves have several uses. Villagers use them in the walls of houses and in the weaving of mats. They use the stems of the leaves for brooms and kite frames. Nothing from "the tree of life" is wasted.

Elberto's nipa hut. When tied together, leaves of the nipa tree act as the roof and walls of the hut.

Elberto's Nipa Hut

Elberto's home is called a "nipa hut" because it is built mostly from the nipa palm tree. The floor, usually made of bamboo, is high above the ground so it will not be ruined by humidity and high tides. The huts are frail, so during a typhoon, villagers take refuge in the church. In 1985, the typhoons were bad and destroyed mango trees and basketball posts. Elberto's mother worries. Their house is only about 20 yards (18 m) from the sea, and during a typhoon, the sea moves closer.

The verandah. It is used as a guest room, workroom, and playroom. In the rainy season, the roof leaks, so the family must re-thatch the roof every two years.

A large nipa hut surrounded by shrubs. Nipa huts are airy and are fine for escaping the tropical heat.

Bundles of nipa palms for sale.

Seven years ago, relatives helped Elberto's family build their home. First they built a frame of bamboo poles. Then they thatched the roof with nipa leaves. Finally, they built the walls and the front.

Then they fixed the inside of the hut. The first room they finished was the kitchen. The second was the living room, where the whole family sleeps on straw mats. Then they added a storeroom and a porch. The toilet, an outhouse, is in the back yard. One day Elberto's parents will plant a vegetable garden. Mario sent money from Manila, so they bought electric lights. But many villagers use candles or kerosene lamps.

Two boys raise the Philippine flag.

School

Elberto walks to the nearby public elementary school. He is in class 2 of the 6th grade. Of the 44 children in his class only 30 attend today. Five boys who have been fishing in the morning arrive after lunch.

The pupils in one grade can be all ages. One girl, Josefina, is 16. She was out of school working for several years. Only recently has she returned. Once Elberto had to leave school, too. His mother was ill, and he had to do housework. It is common for children to leave school so they can help support the family.

A girl leads the pledge of allegiance.

Students in the Philippines attend only six years of elementary school. Some go on to four years of high school, and a few go on to the university or vocational school. But many never graduate from elementary school.

On nice days, the students gather at half past seven in the morning. They raise the flag and pledge allegiance to their country. They also pledge their duties as family members, as pupils, and as good citizens. Then they exercise.

There are 70 languages in the Philippines. But in school the teachers use English and Pilipino, the official languages. Pilipino is also known as Tagalog. In Elberto's area people also speak a language called Waray-waray.

Class 2 of the 6th grade with Mrs. Benito, the teacher. Elberto is kneeling in front, fourth from the left.

Elberto writes his lesson on notebook paper.

First the students do arithmetic. They are learning to multiply and divide. Elberto has been absent from school a long time, so he is not sure how to do the calculations. The second lesson is English. Mrs. Benito, the teacher, says, "Those who can read the poem on the blackboard, raise your hands." Many hands shoot up. She chooses Elberto to read the poem, which is called "The Sea." He reads with lots of energy, probably because he likes rowing on the sea.

Pictures Elberto drew in art class.

Sometimes Filipino students, like students in other lands, like to daydream!

Elberto also likes the poem because it reminds him of the sad and peaceful feelings he sometimes has when he is fishing:

> Why does the sea laugh, Mother,
> As it glints beneath the sun?
>
> It is thinking of the joys, my child,
> That it wishes everyone.
>
> Why does it sob so, Mother,
> As it breaks on the rocky shore?
>
> It recalls the sorrow of the world
> And sadness forevermore.
>
> Why is the sea so peaceful, Mother,
> As if it were fast asleep?
>
> It would give you a restful heart, dearest child,
> The comforts of the deep.

Mrs. Benito does multiplication on the blackboard.

Mrs. Benito writes on the blackboard because there are not enough books for everyone. The students copy the lesson into their notebooks. Children in 3rd grade and below write with pencils. The older children use ballpoint pens. After arithmetic and English, the students take a half-hour break. They rush to the sari sari store for treats. The ice candy seller tries to get their attention, too, by ringing his bell.

A page from a Pilipino language textbook.

After recess, the children study music. There are no instruments, so the children sing — loudly. Next they study Pilipino, one of Elberto's favorite subjects. After the four morning classes, the children have lunch. They have an hour break, so everyone can go home for lunch. Then they return to study science. Again, there are no textbooks, so the teacher must write on the blackboard.

Finally, the children study homemaking. The teacher describes types of cloth and the students sew. Elberto learns to patch his trousers. Next week, they will learn to cook. This pleases the children, who look forward to cooking rice and taro leaves in coconut milk. Like many children, Elberto and his friends enjoy cooking just about any food.

Playing baseball after school. These children are using their sandals for a catcher's mitt and for home plate.

After School Fun

Monday through Friday, the students come to school at 7:30 a.m. At 3:50 p.m., they may leave school. But some children like to stay and play baseball. The children are always sure to have a ball and bat. But sometimes they need to use rubber sandals for the catcher's mitt and for home plate. Other children play jump rope with an elastic cord.

Lately, the children have been skipping school. This worries Mrs. Benito. A video house has been built near San Roque. The children have been working during school hours so they can pay to see videos at night. Elberto sees these shows, too, but he does not tell his mother. She would worry because the movies are violent. Other adults in the village have started to worry about their children.

Some students play jump rope with an elastic cord.

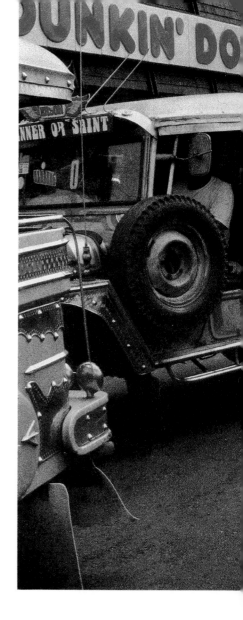

A Trip to Tacloban City

One day some neighbors take Elberto to Tacloban City. Tacloban is just one hour from San Roque by "jeepney." Even so, this is only Elberto's first visit. A jeepney is a kind of bus. It is made by lengthening a jeep so it holds over 10 passengers. Owners cover their jeepneys with chrome pieces of all kinds and with tassles, pictures, and plastic streamers in all colors of the rainbow.

With a population of around 80,000, Tacloban is much bigger than San Roque. In fact, Tacloban is Leyte's largest city. The trip is fun for Elberto. When he gets home, he is quite excited, and he tells his family all about it: "I walked all around the city and saw a movie theater with lots of photographs outside. But I didn't get to see the movie."

A "jeepney." It is decorated in many colors with streamers, pictures, and chrome attachments.

Posters of movie stars at the theater.

Buying grilled meat on a stick. Many food stalls do a fine business in the city.

Elberto may not have seen any movies, but he did look inside a hotel. He thought it was a super building. It had soft beds he could sink into. A soft fluffy bed looks much more comfortable than Elberto's mat. But a bed like that is expensive.

Tacloban has many shops and people. Elberto stops at a street stall to get grilled meat on a stick. The size of Tacloban scares him. But he still wants to see Manila, where Mario lives, even though it is even bigger than Tacloban.

Harvesting rice.

Farming Around San Roque

In the countryside around San Roque are farms. Elberto and his brother take a customer out to one in their pedicab. Elberto likes to watch people working in the fields. His mother is from a farm family. Most Filipinos work on farms, but most farmers work for wealthy landowners. Like most fishermen, the farmers live poor lives.

A rice-cleaning mill. During the rainy season, it is a fine day when the sun shines for drying rice.

The carabao, or water buffalo, a valuable animal in the fields.

Rice, the nation's biggest crop, is grown in the paddy fields. Coconuts and sugar cane are also farming products, and many farmhouses are surrounded by coconut and banana trees. Elberto knows working in the fields is hard work. He'd rather fish.

Farmers use strong, large water buffaloes to plow their paddy fields. During the rainy season, the farmers take advantage of any dry day they get and use it to dry out their rice.

Fernando helps in the field.

Elberto knows a boy named Fernando. Fernando is nine years old, and he works in the field. His parents also work in the fields, and they receive only meals and a small wage for their day's labors. Like Elberto and other children, Fernando skips school during the busy season to earn money. He cuts rice, gathers the rice cut by others, and ties it into sheaves. The adults carry these sheaves on their heads. The workers like to break for lunch, which they cook themselves. They eat as much as they like.

Pictures of the Virgin Mary and young Jesus on the wall.

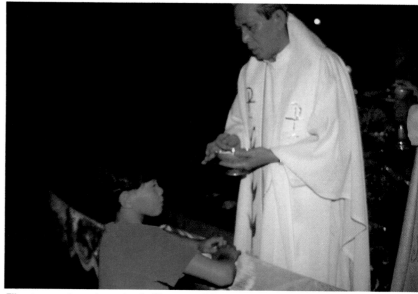

Elberto receives the priest's Christmas blessing.

Christmas in San Roque

Christmas is a festive holiday in the village, and everyone has anxiously awaited its arrival. Now, at last, Christmas is here. Elberto's parents move the table to the living room, and neighborhood children share the family feast. For this special occasion, the plastic dishes are put away, and everyone eats on china plates. There is a new tablecloth, too. The feast includes rice, fried noodles, bean-jam cake, and steamed potato and taro.

A church in Manila.

A giant Christmas tree in Manila.

The Spaniards brought Catholicism to the Philippines. Now
most Filipinos are Catholic, and their nation is the largest
Catholic country in Southeast Asia. Even poor families have a
figure of the Virgin Mary in the best corner of their homes.
Elberto and his family go to Mass in their best clothes.
Neighbors give them candy and cakes.

When the fun of Christmas has passed, Elberto thinks about the future. He decides that when he graduates from high school, he will get a job on a foreign boat. He knows a lot about the sea, and he will work hard, grow rich, and build a log house for his family. He will fill this with soft beds like those he saw in Tacloban. His parents and brothers and sisters will sleep well on such soft beds. So will Elberto.

On Christmas, the children wear their best clothes.

Children enjoy the waters at sunset in Manila Bay.

FOR YOUR INFORMATION: the Philippines

Official Name: Republic of the Philippines

Capital: Manila (Quezon City)

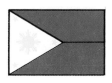

History

The Pre-Spanish Period (Prehistory to 1521)

For some time, the Negritos were believed to be the first people on the islands. They came from Borneo and Sumatra 30,000 years ago, when some of the islands were still connected by land. But now archaeologists suspect that 50,000 years ago an older primitive people were living on the island of Palawan and possibly in the center of Luzon when the Negritos arrived. In the 14th century, Malayo-Polynesian people came from the south, some by land bridges and some by boats called *barangays*. In their villages, also called *barangays*, chieftains called *datus* ruled tribes made up of family members. In the 9th century, Chinese merchants arrived to trade with rather than rule the islanders, and in the 14th century, Arabs moved into the south and brought Islam to the islands. But the Malays were the largest group when the Spanish arrived in the 16th century.

The Spanish Period (1521-1898)

In 1521, the Spanish explorer Ferdinand Magellan invaded the islands. He was killed in a skirmish with Lapu-Lapu, a chieftain on Mactan Island. Miguel Lopez de Legazpi claimed the islands in 1565 and named them after King Philip II of Spain. The Spanish ruled for 377 years and converted many islanders to the Roman Catholic faith. They took power from the various chieftains, taxed the people, and made the Roman Catholic clergy politically powerful by giving them great tracts of land.

During this period, the Spaniards used the islands as a port for trade between China and Mexico, then a colony called "New Spain." Ships would arrive in the islands with goods from China, and some items would be traded for Philippine goods. The ships would then move on to trade in Mexico. Then the ships would reverse their route and go from Mexico to the Philippines to China, trading at each place. The Spanish made lots of money. Filipinos didn't — possibly because the Spanish were more concerned about the economy of Mexico than that of the Philippines.

Many Filipinos resisted Spanish rule, launching over 100 revolts. In 1896, José Rizal, Andrés Bonafacia, and Emilio Aquinaldo led an uprising that the Spanish put down by 1897. The non-violent scholar Rizal was arrested on false charges and put to death; now Filipinos consider him their national hero. In 1899, Aquinaldo became president of the new Philippine Republic. This turned out to be a temporary post, for soon the US would be directing the islands' affairs.

The American Period (1898-1946)

In 1898, the US and Spain battled over Cuba. The Spanish lost. As part of their payment, they surrendered the Philippines to the US. Aquinaldo and other Filipinos had taken the side of the US against Spain, but later fought the US when the islands were not given independence. The three-year war that followed, which Filipinos call The Philippine-American War, ended in 1902 when Aquinaldo swore allegiance to the US. From then until 1941, the US helped Filipinos develop educational and legal systems and improve sanitation and health programs, which decreased mortality and raised the standard of living for many.

In 1935 Manuel Quezon was named the first president of the Commonwealth. He was to have guided the country to full independence by 1945. But in 1941, during World War II, the Japanese invaded the islands. Some believe as many as 2.5 million Filipinos died during the Japanese occupation. In 1944, the US, under General Douglas MacArthur, returned to the islands, and on July 4, 1946, the islands declared themselves the Republic of the Philippines, with Manuel A. Roxas as their first president. But the people celebrate June 12, the day they broke with Spain, as their real independence day.

After Independence (1946-present)

Since World War II, Philippine presidents have developed programs to solve the social and economic problems caused by the war and by years of foreign rule. Some people believe the US has been too involved in the Philippine economy, so the Republic now trades with the Japanese and Europeans. Filipinos also want their leaders to strengthen ties with other Asian neighbors and to reform economic and social programs within the country. Even now, 70% of the Filipinos live below the poverty level.

A Manila police officer.

Government

After 400 Years of Colonial Rule

The Philippines have the misfortune of being a handy stopping-off point between Eastern and Western countries. This has made it vulnerable to invasion by anyone passing through, whether explorers, traders, missionaries, or military. So Filipinos have had trouble establishing their own stable government. Before 1521, tribal chiefs ruled democratically in small villages. From 1521 until 1945, over 400 years, Spain, the US, or Japan controlled the lives of the Filipinos. So the story of government in the Philippines has been the story of a people trying to rule themselves without outside interference.

Today, the US government has an agreement to maintain Clark Air Base and Subic Naval Base on the islands until 1991. So about 13,500 Americans live on the islands, and often military personnel from the US Navy's Seventh Fleet temporarily visit. These military people have about 20,000 spouses and children with them. Nearly 1000 civilians working at the bases also live there.

Government Under Marcos

The Philippine constitution, adopted in 1945 and based on the US model, provides for legislative, judicial, and executive branches of government. Later amendments, however, produced a semi-parliamentary system in which two-thirds of the president's cabinet are also members of the legislature. This leaves only one-third of the seats for people who might oppose the president. A 1981 amendment gave increased powers to the president — then Ferdinand E. Marcos. This amendment made him head of the government and of the army and allowed him to appoint the prime minister, heads of bureaus, judges in the Supreme Court and lower courts, and the more powerful officers in the armed forces. Many people believe Marcos engineered these amendments to increase his power. In 1972 he declared martial law so that he could remain in power without holding elections.

By declaring martial law, a leader can suspend the rights given to citizens by the constitution. After 1972, radio and television stations, newspapers, and magazines could publish only what Marcos wanted them to. People could not criticize his policies and were not allowed to move about freely or meet in groups that might challenge his government. During the eight years of martial law, he introduced the New Society Movement, a group that further restricted civil liberties.

Aquino and the Opposition to Marcos

In 1981, elections were held and members of the New Society Movement, including Marcos, won 80-90% of the votes. Some Filipinos suspected the elections were not honest. The two major parties, the Liberals and the Nacionalistas, remained inactive during much of this period. But eventually these opposition parties, as well as The United Nationalist Democratic Organization (UNIDO) and the PDP-Laban party, challenged the Marcos government. Two other parties seeking a voice in government have been the Moro National Liberation Front (MNLF), a group representing Muslims, and the New People's Army (CCP-NPA), a Communist group.

In 1983, the assassination of Benigno Aquino, Jr., a Marcos opponent, caused unrest among the people, who asked that elections be held to challenge Marcos' presidency. On February 7, 1986, Marcos won. But his opponent, Mrs. Corazon C. (Cory) Aquino, who was backed by both the UNIDO and PDP-Laban parties, claimed election fraud. The National Movement for Free Elections, the Bishops Conference, and many foreign countries refused to recognize Marcos. On February

21, 1986, military leaders Juan Ponce Enrile and Fidel Ramos led a military mutiny. Filipino citizens took to the streets and protected soldiers who had turned against Marcos. Marcos then left the country, and Corazon Aquino, widow of the slain senator, became the first woman president of the Philippines. In February, 1987, the Philippine people voted for a new national constitution. The constitution, which won by a huge margin, confirms Aquino as president until 1992. Many of its provisions reform policies dictated by Marcos. The constitution prohibits presidents from succeeding themselves in office and from appointing family members to government positions. It also limits the role of the military in government, re-establishes a US-style two-house Congress, and guarantees the right to form workers' unions and the right to a fair trial. The new constitution allows the US to keep its major military bases in the Philippines but bans the presence of nuclear weapons.

Language

The national language of the islands is Pilipino, based on *Tagalog*, the dialect of the Tagalog people of Manila and South Luzon. Newspapers, TV, schools, and people meeting from different regions all use Pilipino as a common language. But at least 80 other regional languages do not resemble one another at all. Because the US helped develop the government and schools, English is used in those institutions as well as in business, and Filipinos are proud of being the third largest English-speaking country in the world.

Population and Ethnic Groups

Some Filipinos are descendants of the dark-skinned Negritos; some are brown-skinned Malays; some are Chinese; and some are *mestizo*, people with Spanish and American blood. Of the 80 peoples that make up the Philippines' population of 52 million, the Malays and Chinese are the largest groups.

In the mountains of northern Luzon are primitive tribes. They number over 200,000 people in all and range up and down the mountains. Some of these tribes have impressed Western archaeologists with architecture that may go back over 500 years. The Ifugao, in particular, excel at building terraces into the mountains for their rice paddies. They have built terraces and watering systems rising 8000 ft (2450 m) up the mountains.

Westerners are also excited by the discovery of a new tribe in 1971. This group, called the Tasaday, lives in caves on southern Mindanao. When discovered, there were only about 25 members in the tribe and 19 of them were male, so it appears that when a man wants to marry, he must find a woman from another tribe. Unlike the tribes in northern Luzon, this group is gentle. It does not understand hate. Neither does it have organized systems as the other tribes do: no rituals or art forms or religious beliefs or kin-group legal systems. The Tasaday simply live harmoniously in the forest, eating grubs, crabs, and yams, although Westerners have shown them how to trap animals. Before the Westerners came, deer did not run from the Tasaday, but now they do, probably because the tribe has learned to hunt them. 51

A fresh food market in Manila.

Some archaeologists believe that 700-900 years ago, the Tasaday were connected to a larger tribal group but became separated and have lived in peaceful isolation ever since.

For the most part, men and women are economic and legal equals in the Philippines. This is true among both the mountain people and Filipinos from the "lowlands," the civilized area where most Filipinos live. Women as well as men inherit property and take on many of the same jobs that men do, although in the tribes, when someone must leave the rice fields and children to hunt for meat, it is usually the men who leave. In the cities, Filipino women hold jobs in government, business, and the professions. But usually women are also responsible for the home, the children, and taking care of family finances.

Religion

About 83% of the people are Catholic, 9% Protestant, 5% Muslim, and 3% other religions. Filipinos readily adopt ideas from other faiths, so varieties of beliefs occur. The Muslims of Southern Mindanao, proud of resisting Spanish Catholicism, have schools in which the Islamic religion is taught using Arabic language and writing. The Moro National Liberation Front (MNLF) wants the islands of Mindanao, Basilan, Sulu, and Palawan to break from the Christian-dominated Philippine government and become an independent Muslim state. Before World War II, Muslims had held sway on these islands, but after the war, Christians moved in and Muslims now make up only about 25% of the population. Some Filipinos believe that the MNLF does not really want a separate religious state. They think Muslims chiefly want an end to discrimination against Muslims and the right to control once again their own land.

Performing Arts and Fine Arts

The arts in the Philippines reflect the influence of its many ethnic groups and of the Spanish and US colonizers.

Dance

Traditional Filipino dance is based on Malay, Muslim, and Spanish influences. Some dances reflect the interest in nature held by primitive tribes on the islands. Others recall war and funeral rites. Other forms of dance are popular, too. Two organizations that support classical ballet and modern dance are the National Ballet Federation and the Cultural Center Modern Dance Group.

In 1987 the Philippine Educational Theater Association brought to North America a production combining dance, music, and drama called *dula-tula*. This group wanted to recreate a feel for the political, economic, and cultural conditions that led to the historic and dramatic overthrow of Ferdinand Marcos in 1986. The name of the production was "An Oath to Freedom."

Music

Some music of the Philippines reminds listeners of Western music. Traditional *kundiman* sounds similar to German folk songs; the *zarzuela* is supposedly based on

Italian opera; and rock stars play the "Pinoy sound," a blend of Western and Filipino elements. Rock groups translate European and English lyrics into Pilipino or Taglish (a blend of Tagalog and English). The National Folk Arts Center also provides scholarships for those wishing to pursue classical music.

But Filipinos also create music that more directly reflects their culture. The Popular Music Foundation of the Philippines supports composers who create original pieces in Pilipino. And Filipinos still enjoy older ethnic forms of music that contrast sharply with Western music. The music of Islamic and native religions uses instruments such as Muslim gongs (*kulintang*), a kind of two-stringed lute (the *hagalong*), a fiddle with human hair for strings (the *git-git*), the jew's harp (the *dubing*), and the nose flute.

Theater

Theatergoers in the Philippines can see a wide variety of plays, including Western, experimental, and street theater; popular plays; plays spoken in Tagalog; and religious plays. Many of the theaters are in Manila, the capital city. Here one may enjoy a variety of plays in a variety of settings. One theater, called the Rajah Sulayman Theater, is an open courtyard in Fort Santiago. José Rizal, the national hero, was held in this fort before being put to death. It also held American and Filipino soldiers in World War II. During fiestas Filipinos see street theater such as the *comedia* or *moro-moro*, a play about the conflict between Christians and non-Christians. The fiesta grew from passion plays, plays about Christ's crucifixion. Fiesta street theater is often religious, and audiences usually participate in performances.

Decorating for a fiesta in Manila.

Film

For many years, Filipinos relied on Hollywood for films. Now the fourth largest producer of movies in the world, the Republic encourages both commercial and independent filmmaking. The Manila International Film Festival gives independent

Filipino filmmakers a chance to show their work, and the Experimental Cinema of the Philippines helps fund film projects.

Literature

For centuries, Filipinos have had an oral tradition of stories passed on by word-of-mouth. When the Spaniards arrived, Filipinos around Manila Bay also had a local script. Based on ancient Indian languages, this script lasted another 200 years. Now only scholars can read and write it. The Philippines' first printed book was in Spanish, but books are now printed in English and Pilipino. With their interest in establishing a national identity, writers often work in Pilipino, the national language. Because the islands enjoy the highest literacy rate in Asia, libraries are filled with works by Filipinos. One poet, José Garcia Villa, named a National Artist in 1973, teaches a poetry workshop at the New School in New York.

Painting and Sculpture

In 1821, the Filipino Academy of Painting began. Spanish themes and techniques dominated the Academy in the years that followed, and two Filipino painters, Juan Luna and Felix Resureccion Hidalgo, won prizes in 1884 at the Madrid Exposition in Spain. For many years the government urged painters to create paintings that are in the style called "social realism." In this style, works encourage people to hold certain ideas about society and history. But more recently painters are expressing their own ideas through their work. In Manila one can see their work in the Museum of Philippine Contemporary Art.

Parks are filled with statues dedicated to heroes from Philippine history. One of the most popular sculptors of such work was Guillermo Tolentino. His bronze monuments concerning events in Philippine history are so popular that he became a cultural hero before his death in 1976.

Land

With a total land area of about 115,000 sq miles (300,000 sq km), the Philippines are about the size of Arizona, or about half the size of Saskatchewan. It is a country of 7100 islands and islets nestled between the warm tropical waters of the Pacific and the South China Sea. The southernmost island group of Tawitawi is only 15 miles (24 km) from Malaysian Borneo, and the northernmost part of the chain, the Batan Islands, is 100 miles (161 km) south of Taiwan. Imagine a chain of mountains running north to south about 1000 miles, but with only the tips of the mountains showing because the seas have climbed up the slopes.

Over 90% of the total land area is represented by only 11 islands. The two largest islands are Luzon and Mindanao. A collection of smaller inhabited islands makes up the third largest region, the Visayas. On some islands are volcanoes, some still active. On occasion, destructive earthquakes also strike the islands.

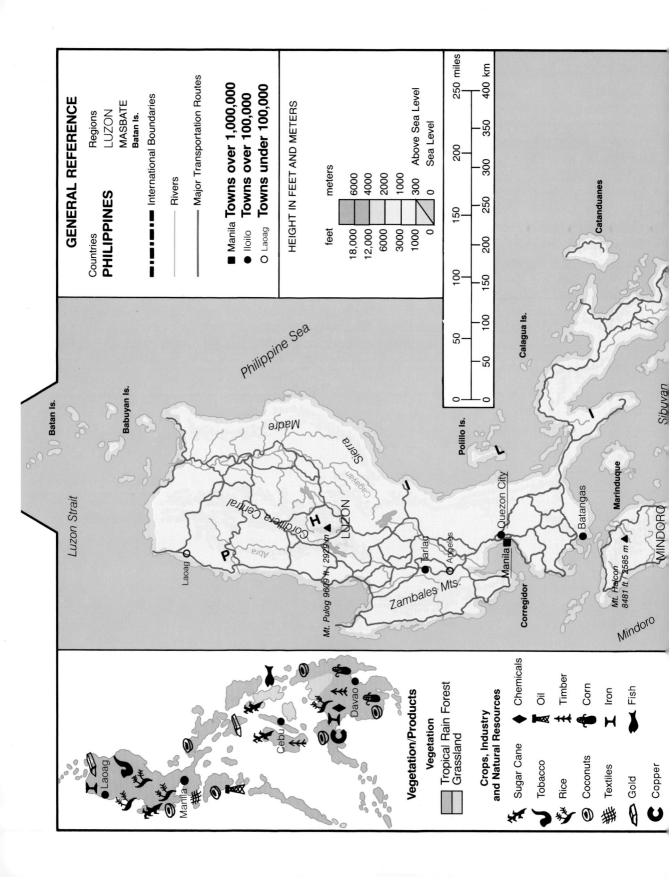

GENERAL REFERENCE

Countries
PHILIPPINES

Regions
LUZON
MASBATE
Batan Is.

▬▪▬▪ International Boundaries

Rivers

Major Transportation Routes

■ Manila **Towns over 1,000,000**
● Iloilo **Towns over 100,000**
○ Laoag **Towns under 100,000**

HEIGHT IN FEET AND METERS

feet	meters
18,000	6000
12,000	4000
6000	2000
3000	1000
1000	300
0	0

Above Sea Level

Sea Level

0   50   100   150   200   250 miles

0   50   100   150   200   250   300   350   400 km

Batan Is.

Babuyan Is.

Luzon Strait

Philippine Sea

Sierra Madre

Cagayan

Cordillera Central

Abra

Laoag ○

P

H
▲ Mt. Pulog 9609 ft / 2929 m

LUZON

I

Zambales Mts.

Tarlac ●

Angeles ○

Corregidor

Manila ■

Quezon City ●

Polillo Is.

L

Calagua Is.

Catanduanes

I

Batangas ●

Marinduque

Mt. Halcon
8481 ft / 2585 m ▲

MINDORO

Mindoro

Sibuyan

Vegetation/Products

Vegetation

▨ Tropical Rain Forest
▨ Grassland

Crops, Industry and Natural Resources

Sugar Cane	◆ Chemicals		
Tobacco	🏭 Oil		
Rice	🌲 Timber		
◉ Coconuts	Corn		
🌾 Textiles	I Iron		
Gold	🐟 Fish		
C Copper			

Laoag ●

Manila ●

Cebu ●

Davao ●

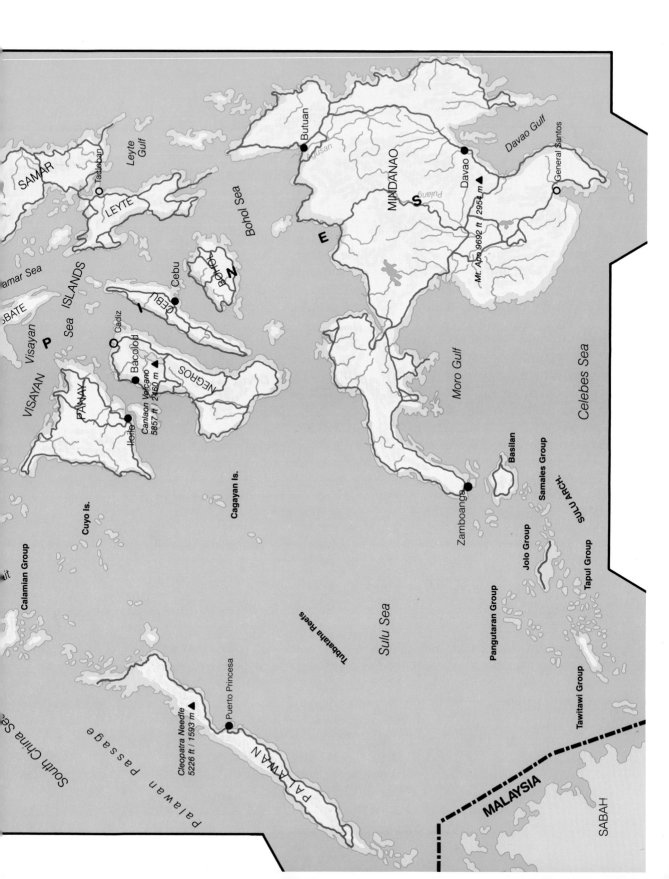

Climate

Filipinos enjoy a lush, green, tropical climate of about 70-80° F (21-27° C) all year. What they do not enjoy is being in a typhoon belt. Typhoons are tropical storms of powerful winds and rain that strike about five times a year, destroying property and life. The southern part of the country, fortunately, has less turbulent weather. The rainy season is from about June to November and the dry season from March through May.

Industry, Agriculture, and Natural Resources

Of the 115,000 sq miles (298,000 sq km) in the Philippines, 30% are farmed, and 30% are swampy and often used for fish ponds. Farmers grow coffee, sugar, coconuts, rice, corn, pineapples, and bananas. Mindanao is by far the most fertile island, producing most of the nation's agricultural products. One saying even has it that you can stick your finger into the ground in Mindanao and the finger will grow.

The mountains covering about 53% of the Republic's land are a source of timber and minerals. Forests are crucial to the economy because they produce timber for export. Recently, the government began a conservation program to protect forests from reckless lumbering. The mountains also yield valuable minerals. The major mineral resources are iron, cobalt, silver, gold, petroleum, chromite, nickel, and copper. Mindanao is also the richest island for the Republic's mineral resources. Other natural products of the Philippines include tuna and prawns from the sea. These are needed to feed the Filipino people and are not generally exported.

From about 1900 to 1940, when the US occupied the Philippines, Filipinos built textile and cigar/cigarette factories as well as sawmills, coconut oil mills, fish canneries, sugar processing plants, and alcohol distilleries. More recently, they have been assembling electronic items and chemicals for export. In the past, over half the Filipinos earned their living in agriculture, but very shortly more will be working in industry.

During the American colonization, Filipinos had a special trade agreement with the US. The agreement meant that Filipinos did most of their trading with the US and became dependent on it as a market. Now the Republic has expanded its trading partners to include Japan and the European Economic Community.

Education

There are about 39,000 public and 3000 private schools in the Philippines. Everyone must attend school for six years, and 95% of the Filipinos do complete grade 6. Other education is not required, so only 57% complete higher forms of education. About 88% of the population can read and write. In Manila, the rate is 92%. About 1200 public and private colleges serve about 1.5 million students, 40% of them in Metro Manila.

Sports and Recreation

Gambling and betting are common activities in the Philippines, so games will often have lively groups of people shouting from the sidelines in support of the side they have placed their money on.

Filipinos love basketball, "the tall man's game." Nearly every village contains a statue of José Rizal (the national hero), a platform for political rallies, and a basketball court. Even the poorest Filipinos can play. They just make a hoop out of something handy around the house and hang it on a coconut tree. Every year, Filipinos hold amateur and professional tournaments.

Even more important to the men, perhaps, is the cockfight, called *tupada* or *sabong*. Some people believe this to be too violent a sport. In each town, owners take their fighting cocks to an area set aside for contests and pit the birds against one another. The birds wear blades called "spurs" on their legs and with these slash one another. Onlookers place bets to see which bird will win and usually become quite excited during these battles, cheering their favorite on to victory.

The Jai Alai Fronton in Manila is one of the few outside Spain. It is the first in Asia. Players on each team use wicker baskets shaped like half-circles to scoop and throw the ball against a wall. Action is fast and the players agile. As usual in the Philippines, gambling among the spectators occurs between each game.

A quieter interest of the people is chess. Since World War II Filipinos have been Asia's best chess players in international competitions. Thousands of Filipinos play in clubs, corner stores, barber shops, and anywhere else they can safely set up a board. Two famous players are Eugene Torre, a grandmaster, and Rosendo Balinas. In 1978, Baguio City hosted the world chess championships, the first time competitions were held in the East.

Currency

The smallest unit of currency is the *centavo*. One hundred of these equal a *peso*. Paper notes are in denominations of 100, 50, 20, 10, 5, and 2 pesos. Coins are in denominations of 2 and 5 peso, and 1, 5, 10, 25, and 50 centavo.

Manila

In 1948, Quezon City, which is within the Manila area, was chosen as the capital of the Republic. But most people refer to Manila as the capital. Nearly 7 million people live in Manila, on the southern tip of Luzon. The site of Asian offices of many international organizations, Manila is also the major commercial center and port of the islands. It has a natural crescent-shaped harbor that has always made the city appealing to traders. Now the city is so developed that four more cities and 13 municipalities are included in the larger area called Metro Manila.

In the center of the city are tall modern buildings, and in some neighborhoods are houses that look like palaces. Beautiful parks and monuments honor national heroes. Residents and tourists visit these places as well as the many theaters and restaurants in the city. Also located here are publishing houses of newspapers and magazines. The city's industry, business, and trade attract professional Filipinos with degrees in law, medicine, and teaching.

But the city also attracts the poor who move to Manila hoping to find some kind of work. Like many large cities in developing nations, Manila has not been able to find space or jobs for all of these people. So the job-seekers live in slums: Houses have no gas, electricity, running water, or toilets. About 80% of the slum children are malnourished. Many appear on the streets selling gum and cigarettes to make some money.

Many people who come to Manila live in slums like these.

Filipinos in North America

Many Filipinos have migrated to North America, especially to the US, which has been involved in Philippine affairs since 1898. In 1985 alone, over 37,000 Filipinos applied for permanent residence in the US, and over 2300 applied for student permits. In the same year, around 3000 Filipinos applied for permanent status in Canada and over 2500 applied for student status. Some who emigrate to Canada become Canadian citizens and *then* come to the US. Because many more Asians than Westerners immigrate to the United States, US immigration quotas favor Canadian applicants.

In both the US and Canada, the largest Filipino communities are in each country's three largest cities: New York, Los Angeles, and Chicago; and Toronto, Vancouver, and Montreal. These cities are most popular primarily because they already have large Filipino populations and also because they are the best known North American cities. Many Filipinos in North America have become very productive members of US and Canadian society. Many go into the sciences and the various medical professions. Most major North American cities have their share of Filipino physicians and nurses. In Chicago alone, for example, there are over 1000 Filipino nurses.

More Books About the Philippines

Here are more books about the Philippines. If you are interested in them, check your library. Some may be helpful in doing research for the "Things to Do" projects that follow.

The Land and People of the Philippines. Nance (Lippincott)
The Philippines. Lepthien (Childrens Press)
The Philippines. Roland (Macmillan)
The Philippines (A First Book). Poole (Franklin Watts)

Glossary of Useful Pilipino Terms

binibini (bee-nee-BEE-nee) . . . . Miss
Filipina (fil-ih-PEEN-ah) . . . . a woman from the Philippines
Filipino (fil-ih-PEEN-o) . . . . a man from the Philippines; anyone generally from the Philippines
ginang (GEEN-ahng) . . . . Mrs. or Madam
ginoo (gee-no-OH) . . . . Mr. or Sir
kamusta po kayo? (ka-moo-sta PO ka-YO) How are you?
mabuhay (ma-boo-HI) . . . . welcome or farewell
magandang hapon po
(ma-gahn-DAHNG HA-pone PO) . . . . good afternoon
magandang umaga po
(ma-gahn-DAHNG oo-MA-ga PO) . . . . good morning
moro-moro (mo-ro mo-ro) . . . . religious play performed during fiestas
mestizos (mes-TEE-zos) . . . . (Spanish) Filipinos with Spanish or American blood
oo (oh-oh) . . . . yes
paki (PAY-KEY) . . . . please
salamat po (sa-LA-maht po) . . . . thank you

Things to Do - Research Projects

In February, 1986, a peaceful revolution overturned the repressive Marcos regime and installed the Philippines' first woman president, Corazon Aquino. In February, 1987, a national election was held to decide the status of both the Philippines' constitution and its new president. The rapid pace of events in the Philippines has kept the Republic in the news daily. As you read about developments in the Philippines, or any country, keep in mind the importance of current facts. Some of the research projects that follow need accurate, up-to-date information from current sources. Two publications your library may have will tell you about recent newspaper and magazine articles on many topics:

The Reader's Guide to Periodical Literature
Children's Magazine Guide

For accurate answers to questions about such topics of current interest as the Philippines' attempts to reach a balance of democracy and stability, look up *Philippines* in these two publications. They will lead you to the most up-to-date information from current sources.

1.   The Republic of the Philippines has a constitution drawn up 200 years later than that of the United States, 100 years later than that of Canada. Check the *Reader's Guide to Periodical Literature* or the *Children's Magazine Guide* for articles written about the Philippine constitution of 1987. How is it similar to or different from the one that underlies the government of your country?

2.   How has the location of the Philippines affected its economy and international affairs? Use library resources to find your information.

3.   Many children in the Philippines attend school only part time or stop attending when they are very young. Why is this? How does this affect them as adults?

4.   Find out more about how Christmas is celebrated in the Philippines. How does it compare with Christmas in your country?

5.   After a long and wasteful rule, Ferdinand Marcos was replaced as president of the Philippines by Corazon Aquino. Cory Aquino was not elected, though. Find out more about this change of power.

More Things to Do - Activities

These projects are designed to encourage you to think more about the Philippines. They offer interesting group or individual projects you can do at home or at school.

1.   How far is San Roque from where you live? Using maps, travel guides, travel agents or any other resources you know of, find out how you can get there and how long it would take.

2.   How does your life compare with Elberto's? Write an imaginary letter to him. Explain how you are the same or different.

3.   If you would like a pen pal in the Philippines, write to these people:

International Pen Friends
P.O. Box 65
Brooklyn, New York 11229

4.   Are there people near where you live who make their living by fishing? Find out how their way of life is similar to Elberto's. What are their techniques? What fish do they catch? What are the dangers, both physical and economic?

Index